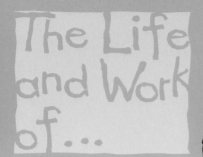

The Life and Work of...

Wassily Kandinsky

Paul Flux

Heinemann
LIBRARY

www.heinemann.co.uk/library
Visit our website to find out more information about Heinemann Library books.

To order:
 Phone 44 (0) 1865 888066
 Send a fax to 44 (0) 1865 314091
 Visit the Heinemann Bookshop at www.heinemann.co.uk/library to browse our catalogue and order online.

First published in Great Britain by Heinemann Library, Halley Court, Jordan Hill, Oxford OX2 8EJ, a division of Reed Educational and Professional Publishing Ltd. Heinemann is a registered trademark of Reed Educational and Professional Publishing Ltd.

OXFORD MELBOURNE AUCKLAND JOHANNESBURG BLANTYRE
GABORONE IBADAN PORTSMOUTH (NH) USA CHICAGO

Designed by Celia Floyd
Illustrations by Sam Thompson
Originated by Ambassador Litho Ltd
Printed and bound in Hong Kong/China

500 759873

ISBN 0 431 09217 6

06 05 04 03 02
10 9 8 7 6 5 4 3 2 1

British Library Cataloguing in Publication Data

Flux, Paul
    The life and work of Wassily Kandinsky
    1. Kandinsky, Wassily, 1866 – 1944
    2. Painters – Russia (Federation) – Biography – Juvenile literature
    3. Painting – Russia (Federation) – Juvenile literature
    I. Title   II. Wassily Kandinsky
    759.7

Acknowledgements

The Publisher would like to thank the following for permission to reproduce photographs:
AKG: p20, Buhrle Collection, Zurich p11, Lenbachlaus, Munich p21; Bridgeman Art Library: p4, Kunstammlung Nordrhein-Westfalen, Dusseldorf p15, Musée National d'Art Moderne, Paris p19, Private Collection p13, Roger Viollet p26, Solomon R Guggenheim Museum, New York p17, Tretyakov Gallery, Moscow, Russia p7; © Foto: Städtische Galerie im Lenbachhaus: p9; Hulton Archive: pp10, 16; RMN: pp5, 22; The Solomon R Guggenheim Foundation, New York: David Heald pp23, 25, 27, 29.

Cover photograph (*Yellow, Red, Blue,* Wassily Kandinsky) reproduced with permission of Bridgeman Art Library/Musée National d'Art Moderne, Paris.

Every effort has been made to contact copyright holders of any material reproduced in this book. Any omissions will be rectified in subsequent printings if notice is given to the Publisher.

Any words appearing in the text in bold, **like this**, are explained in the Glossary.

Contents

Who was Wassily Kandinsky?

Wassily Kandinsky was a Russian painter. He is well known for his **abstract** pictures. He was also a teacher who **inspired** many other artists with his ideas.

Wassily was one of the first artists to paint abstract shapes in bright colours. His paintings don't always look like something from real life. His pictures show new ways of arranging coloured shapes.

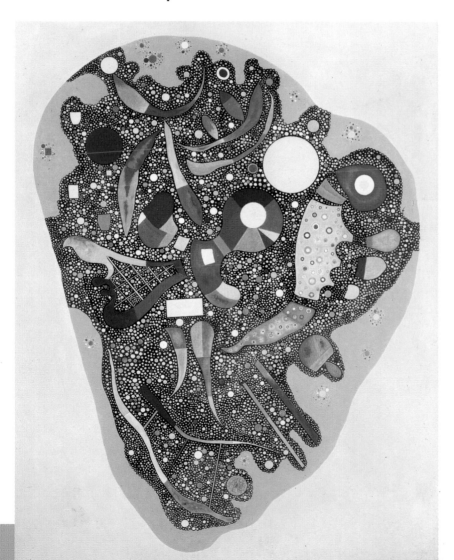

Colourful Ensemble, 1938

Early years

Wassily Kandinsky was born on 4 December 1866, in **Moscow** in Russia. In 1871 his parents **divorced**. Wassily moved to Odessa, also in Russia, to live with his aunt.

In 1889 Wassily visited northern Russia. There he saw art made by the local people. He loved what he saw and began to paint pictures of the places he knew.

The Port of Odessa, 1890

Teaching and learning

In 1892, Wassily married his cousin, Anya Shemiakina. A year later he began to teach at the University of **Moscow**. By 1896 Wassily knew he wanted to be an artist.

In 1900 Wassily began to study art in Munich, in Germany. There he helped start a group of artists called the 'Phalanx'. Wassily made this poster telling people about their first **exhibition**.

Poster for the first Phalanx exhibition, 1901

Experiments with colour

In 1905 Wassily saw a special **exhibition**. All the painters there used strong colours. Henri Matisse was the leader of this group. After this, Wassily became **bolder** in his use of colour.

The Blue Rider, 1903

The rider in this painting is St George, **patron saint** of England. He is riding out to make the world a better place to live in. Wassily wanted his paintings to change the world, too.

A fresh start

Wassily travelled a lot in France and Russia. In 1908 he moved back to Munich, in Germany. There his paintings became more colourful and less **realistic**.

Wassily painted this picture in Murnau, a small town in Germany. He has not tried to show us exactly what he could see. The painting is an **impression** of the view.

Road at Murnau, 1909

New ideas

In 1911 Wassily helped to organize another **exhibition**. All the artists were trying to find exciting ways to paint. Wassily was even **experimenting** with writing poetry.

Composition IV, 1911

Between 1910 and 1939 Wassily painted ten large pictures he called 'Compositions'. This was one of the first **abstract** pictures ever painted. It is made up of shapes and blocks of colour, rather than real objects.

Painting shapes

In 1911 Wassily and Anya were **divorced**. By 1913 Wassily had decided to paint only **abstract** shapes. His paintings were shown in New York, pictured here. People had to look carefully to see what Wassily had painted.

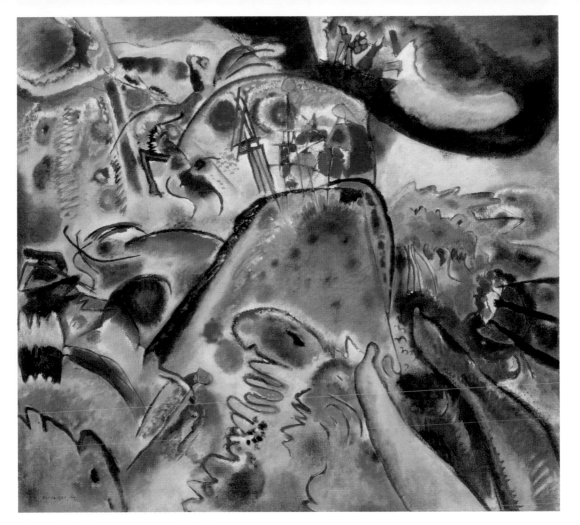

Small Pleasures, 1913

Wassily now tried to fill his pictures with shapes and colours. He said that this painting made him think of the sound of small, falling, drops of water.

Back to Moscow

After **World War I** began in 1914, Wassily returned to **Moscow**. There he met Nina Andreevskaya. They were married in 1917.

When the war ended, Wassily hoped that his homeland would be a good place to live. His paintings were bright and hopeful of the future.

In Grey, 1919

Teaching art

In December 1921 Wassily and Nina left **Moscow** again, to travel to Germany. Wassily began teaching at the **Bauhaus**, a famous art school. He was very excited by this.

This was one of Wassily's last Russian paintings. He was still painting coloured shapes. He often painted circles. He thought these were the most perfect shapes of all.

Red Spot II, 1921

At the Bauhaus

Wassily was very busy with his teaching at the **Bauhaus**, but he also painted a lot. Other artists at the school designed furniture. One of them named this chair after Wassily.

This is one of Wassily's most important pictures from this time. The colours, shapes and spaces between them all balance together perfectly. The other artists Wassily worked with at the Bauhaus **inspired** some of his very best work.

Composition VIII, 1923

The end of the Bauhaus

In 1933 **Adolf Hitler** took power in Germany. He did not like the kind of art the **Bauhaus** was teaching. The Bauhaus closed and most of the teachers moved to other countries.

This was one of the last paintings that Wassily did in Germany. He knew he would not be safe there any longer. In December 1933 he left for Paris.

Decisive Pink, 1932

Living in Paris

In Paris, Wassily tried to make money by selling his paintings. These were difficult years for him. An **exhibition** held in 1937 helped more people to see his work.

In 1939 war broke out once more. In 1940 German soldiers entered Paris, but Wassily stayed in the city. He tried to carry on as normal. He still painted many well known shapes, like the red circle here.

Around the Circle, 1940

Final days

Wassily became ill during the war. He still wanted to find new ways to show his thoughts in his art. He used bright colours and shapes to show what he was feeling.

Twilight, 1943

Wassily died on 13 December 1944. This is one of the last paintings he did. He is remembered for his work on new ways of painting.

Timeline

1866	Wassily Kandinsky is born in **Moscow**, Russia, on 4 December.
1871	Wassily's parents **divorce**. Wassily is brought up by an aunt.
1879	The artist Paul Klee is born.
1886	Wassily studies at Moscow University.
1892	He marries his cousin, Anya Shemiakina.
1893	Wassily teaches at Moscow University.
1896	He begins to study art seriously and moves to Munich, in Germany.
1900	Wassily studies at the Munich Academy of Art.
1901	Wassily helps to start the 'Phalanx' group of artists.
1911	Wassily and his wife are divorced. He helps organize the first '**Blue Rider**' **exhibition**.
1914	**World War I** begins. Wassily escapes to Switzerland and eventually returns to Moscow.
1917	Wassily marries Nina Andreevskaya. They have a son, Vsevdod.
1920	Vsevdod dies.
1921	Wassily and Nina return to Germany.
1922	Wassily starts work at the **Bauhaus** art school.
1923	Wassily has one-man show in New York.
1933	The Bauhaus is closed. Wassily moves to Paris, France.
1939	World War II begins.
1944	Wassily dies in France, aged 78, on 13 December.

Glossary

abstract art which does not try to show people or things. It uses shape and colour to make the picture.

Adolf Hitler German leader from 1933 to 1945

Bauhaus famous art school in Germany

Blue Rider group of artists in Germany, started in 1911, led by Wassily and Franz Marc

bolder braver

divorce to end a marriage

exhibition art on display for people to see

experiment to try things out

impression a sense of what is there

inspired when someone give good ideas to someone else

Moscow capital city of Russia

patron saint holy person that watches over a country

realistic trying to show something as it really is

World War I war in Europe that lasted from 1914 to 1918

More books to read

How Artists Use Shape,
Paul Flux,
Heinemann Library

The Life and Work of Paul Klee,
Sean Connolly,
Heinemann Library

More paintings to see

Cossacks, Wassily Kandinsky,
Tate Gallery, London

Composition IX,
Wassily Kandinsky,
Museum of Modern Art, Paris

Index

Titles in the *Life and Work of* series include:

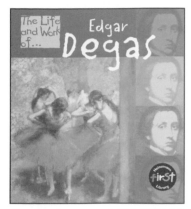

Hardback   0 431 09210 9

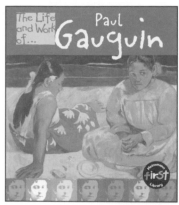

Hardback   0 431 09216 8

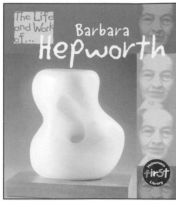

Hardback   0 431 09212 5

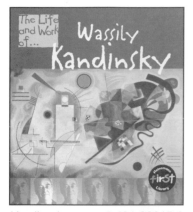

Hardback   0 431 09217 6

Hardback   0 431 09218 4

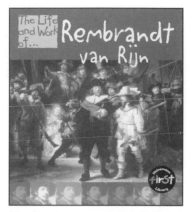

Hardback   0 431 09211 7

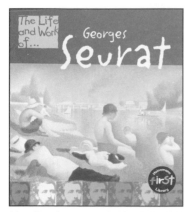

Hardback   0 431 09219 2

Find out about the other titles in this series on our website www.heinemann.co.uk/library